Pysanky Promise

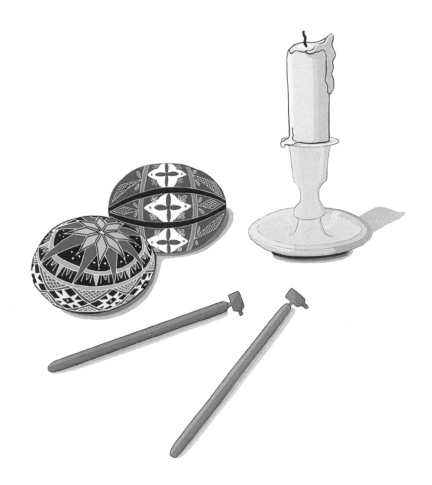

By Cathy Witbeck

Published by Calico Barn Books

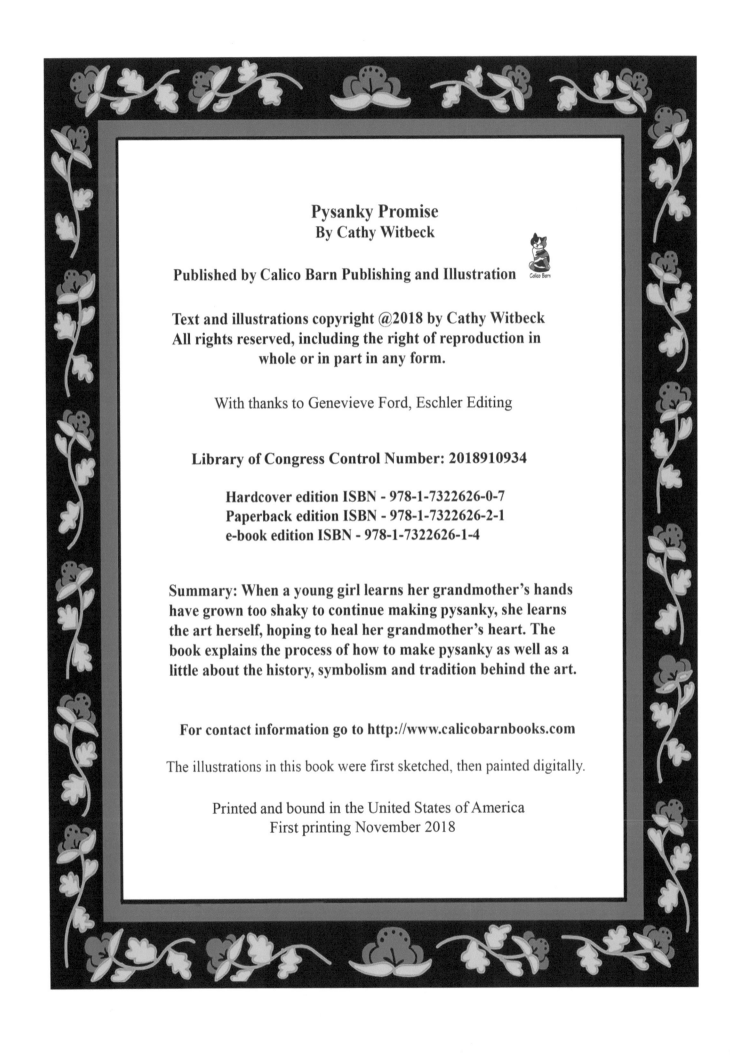

Pysanky Promise
By Cathy Witbeck

Published by Calico Barn Publishing and Illustration

With thanks to Genevieve Ford, Eschler Editing

Library of Congress Control Number: 2018910934

Hardcover edition ISBN - 978-1-7322626-0-7
Paperback edition ISBN - 978-1-7322626-2-1
e-book edition ISBN - 978-1-7322626-1-4

Summary: When a young girl learns her grandmother's hands
have grown too shaky to continue making pysanky, she learns
the art herself, hoping to heal her grandmother's heart. The
book explains the process of how to make pysanky as well as a
little about the history, symbolism and tradition behind the art.

For contact information go to http://www.calicobarnbooks.com

The illustrations in this book were first sketched, then painted digitally.

Printed and bound in the United States of America
First printing November 2018

Pysanky Promise

Dedicated to my parents,
Jerry and Shirley Bennett,
who taught me I could do anything.

With special thanks to my models, Stacie Witbeck, Eleanor Witbeck,
Mindy Bennett, Alice Christensen and Elizabeth Swinyard.

Cathy Witbeck

The dancer spun in a flash of colors. Ribbons flew, and the layers of her skirt flared. Alena clapped and cheered with her family. The smell of perogies, cabbage rolls and kielbasa filled the air. The Ukrainian dance festival was just one of the reasons she loved spring.

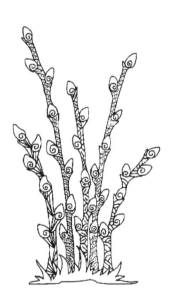

When she got home, Alena looked for her grandmother in the sunroom. Alena knew she loved spring, too. Every year, Grandma grew flowers to make the yard colorful. But, Alena didn't find her working with her plants. Instead, Grandmother stared aimlessly out the window. Something was wrong. Alena bit her lip and slipped away.

She found her mother in the kitchen washing dishes. Alena picked up a dishtowel. "Grandma looks sad," she said. Her heart felt pinched.

Alena's mother nodded. "Last night when Grandma tried to make a pysanka, her hands shook too much to make a good straight line."

"What's wrong with her?" Alena said.

"Grandma's medicine helps her breathe, but it can make her shaky," her mother said. "Making pysanky has always been one of her favorite things."

"Grandma's eggs are so beautiful," Alena said. She'd spent hours looking at the brightly colored eggs in the china cabinet. Grandma only kept a few for the family, she made most of them to give away.

Alena found her father in the barn. The cats were finishing up their food.

"Dad, I don't want Grandma to be sad," Alena said. She kneeled down and picked up a fuzzy kitten. Its fur was soft and warm.

Her father scratched his chin. "I've thought about that. I think Grandma is sad because she feels like she missed her chance to teach you how to make pysanky."

Alena looked up. "Aunt Vierra knows how to make pysanky. Do you think if I offered to help with spring cleaning, she would teach me how to make pysanky? Then I could make a pysanka for Grandma."

Her father smiled and said, "I doubt she would turn down that offer."

On Alena's first day of spring cleaning, she helped Vierra clean light fixtures all morning. It was dusty, but Vierra played music and before long it was lunch time.

Alena could hardly eat. After lunch, pysanky lessons would start. Her heart dropped a little when Vierra said, "Before we make pysanky, I want you to learn a little about their history."

She sat up straighter when Vierra opened a book with brightly colored pages.

"People have been making pysanky for many years. Before Christianity, people believed the egg was a source of power. It held new life and heralded the arrival of spring. To ensure a bountiful harvest, people would decorate an egg and bury it in their field. They painted symbols of life and growth on the egg.

After the ministry of Christ, people added Christian symbols. One of those images is the fish, which is the ancient Greek symbol for Christ."

"The word pysanky is related to the word 'pysaty', which means 'to write.' Pysanky are eggs with a message written on them. The colors and symbols on the eggs have meanings. A spider stands for patience. A horse means prosperity. A rose means beauty and wisdom."

"So, to tell my piano teacher 'thank you for being patient,' I would make her an egg with spiders on it," Alena said, wrinkling her nose.

"Exactly," Vierra said with a chuckle.

"Each color has more than one meaning as well. White can mean purity, light or innocence."

"Orange would be good for Grandma," Alena said.

"You're right," Vierra said. "Grandma is a strong woman. I think she'd like blue, too. She loves the blue sky over the farm."

After they talked about color, Vierra closed the book.

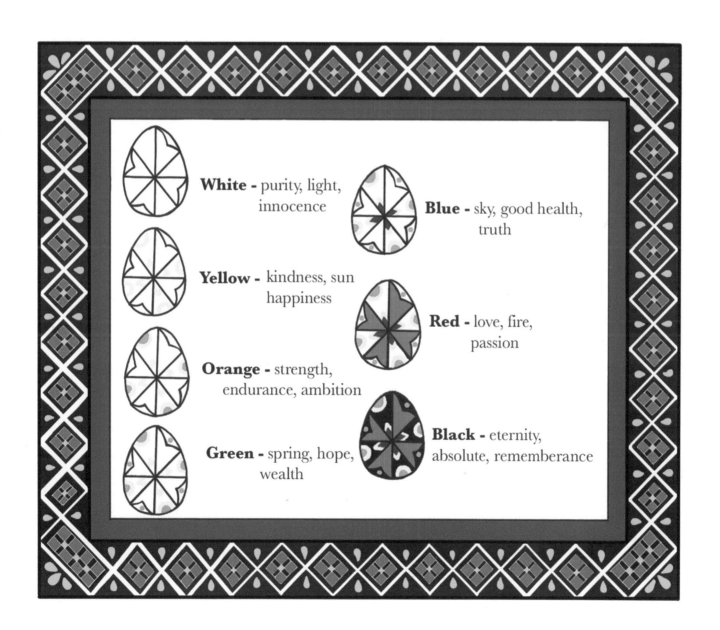

White - purity, light, innocence

Blue - sky, good health, truth

Yellow - kindness, sun happiness

Red - love, fire, passion

Orange - strength, endurance, ambition

Green - spring, hope, wealth

Black - eternity, absolute, rememberance

"Would you like to see how the color goes on the egg?" Vierra asked.

Alena nodded.

Vierra picked up a plastic handle with a tiny brass funnel on the end. "This is a kistka. I heat the metal funnel over a flame. When it's hot enough, I melt the beeswax into the large end. The heated wax flows through the funnel and comes out the tip. Now I use the kistka to draw wax on the egg. The wax sinks into the pores of the shell and keeps the dye from staining that area of the egg."

"The wax won't let the dye in?" Alena said.

"That's right. When I'm done covering the area of the egg I want to stay white, it's time to place the egg in the lightest color of dye. When I take it out, I let it dry before I add more wax. Now that layer of dye is protected. I keep dipping the egg in dye and adding wax until I have the pattern I want."

As Vierra applied the wax and dipped the egg from dye to dye, she told Alena traditional stories about pysanky.

"One legend tells of an evil monster, chained to a hillside. He represents the evil in the world. If only a few pysanky are made, his chains grow loose. But if you make a pysanka for someone with love, his chains tighten and the world is safe for another year."

"His chains will be extra tight when I make grandma's egg," Alena said with a grin.

Covered in wax, the egg looked dull and grey. Vierra held the egg beside a candle flame until the wax looked shiny and wet. With a gentle stroke she wiped off the wax with a tissue. With the wax gone, the bright colors stood out.

Vierra put a small dab of varnish in her hand and rolled the egg until it was coated in a thin film. The varnish made the egg glisten. Then she put it on a rack to dry.

"When the varnish is dry, we'll blow out the egg." Vierra said.

The strong smell of varnish made Alena's nose sting. She was happy to help open some windows.

It had taken so much time to wax the egg, to let it sit in dye and to dry it between dyes, the whole afternoon was spent on one egg. And it wasn't even done yet. At least tomorrow it would be her turn to try.

The next day, it was Alena's turn. She loved the sweet honey smell that drifted up when she took her kistka full of beeswax and warmed it over the flame.

She placed her kistka firmly against the smooth eggshell and began a long line. A large blob of wax dripped from the side of her kistka and made a lumpy shape. Right in the middle of her line.

"Oh no!" She cried. "I've wrecked it."

Vierra patted her on the shoulder. "Use your imagination. Make it into something."

"But it won't look like the pattern."

"No two eggs ever look the same. This is your first try, Alena. Be patient. Remember the spider. She weaves her web with care and it grows more intricate with each strand. Each egg you make will be better than the one before."

Alena picked up her kistka and turned the blob into a daisy.

After several days of practice, Alena was ready to make an egg for her grandmother. She chose symbols and colors she knew her grandmother would love. Wheat for the fields that surrounded the farm and an open rose for the wisdom Grandma shared with the family. She would use orange for strength and blue for the sky.

Like the spider, it took patience. It hadn't looked the way she'd wanted it to on the first try, or the second, but by the third, she knew Grandma would love it.

"There's my girl," Grandma said, when Alena came into her room on Easter morning.

"I have a surprise for you," Alena said. She gently placed the egg into her grandmother's hands.

"Oh, Alena, it's beautiful," she said. "Where did you get it?"

"I helped Aunt Vierra with spring cleaning, and she taught me how to make pysanky."

"You made this?" Grandma's eyes glistened.

Alena had one more surprise. "Someday when I have children, I'm going to teach them how to make pysanky."

Grandma gave her a warm hug. "What a wonderful promise."

The borders of each illustration have pysanky symbols.

Meanings are listed below:

Bird

Fulfilment of wishes

Pussy Willow

The coming of spring

Rose

Loving, caring

Poppy
Favorite flower
of the people

Ram

Dignity, perseverance

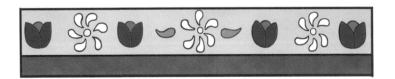

Flower

Beauty, wisdom

Fish

A symbol of Christianity

Diamond

Knowledge

Bees

Diligence

Star

Beauty, perfection

Grapes

Fellowship, continuity

Spider

Patience

Oak leaves and acorns

Persistance, preparation

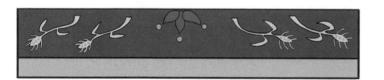

Wheat
Wishes for good health
and a good harvest

Pronunciation Guide:

Pysanka - one egg - peh san keh

Pysanky - more than one - peh san kee

Kistka - kisst ka

*Note - In the legend of the evil monster chained to the hillside, the original story suggests his chains grow tighter with each pysanky made. The author added 'with love' to focus on Alena's relationship with her grandmother.

Alena would like to share her knowledge of pysanky with you. Here are some great websites to visit:

learnpysanky.com - for hints, tips, egg patterns and everything else.

ukrainiangiftshop.com - for basic and advanced supplies.

pysankyusaretreat.com - for people who want to learn.

CPSIA information can be obtained
at www.ICGtesting.com
Printed in the USA
LVHW070305160322
713570LV00002B/68